black artists on art

black artists on art

First printing 1969

Library of Congress Catalog Card Number 76-97788

contemporary crafts publishers ✳ 5616 san vicente boulevard ✳ los angeles, california

Printed in the United States of America

black artists on art

volume 1

Samella S. Lewis
and
Ruth G. Waddy

Design: Howard Lee
Typesetting: Bell & Company, Inc.
Color Separations: Solargraph
Lithography: Anderson, Ritchie & Simon
Copyreading: Charlotte B. Leigh-Taylor

BLACK ARTISTS ON ART is intended to introduce the works and thoughts of a selected number of producing Afro-American artists.

Traditionally it is customary to approach a subject of this nature with some historical justification. I have, however, decided to depart from this tradition because I feel that honest creative expression needs no history or justification.

Many will be surprised to discover the large number of truly creative individuals who are participants outside of the mainstream of art in the United States and the Western world. The fact that these artists are generally unrecognized is not because they are ignored but because they are seldom observed.

The aesthetics of a people is directly tied to the mainstream of their existence. This assumption is a natural consequence which could give rise to resourceful creativeness . . . resourceful creativeness that could provide for differences that might serve as vital accents in the total human scheme. However, one finds that in the United States the "European style aesthetics" commands the art world. Most other cultural orientations are deemed "primitive," quaint or suspect.

The adaptation of this European-imposed style of aesthetics may be regarded more as ancestor worship rather than as a valid system of aesthetics. A truly valid system of aesthetics should be derived from the culture of its inhabitants and should reflect the prevailing spirit of the times in a manner that involves all groups residing within the society. This direction would provide for a concept of relationship that would include both commonalities and differences. Since it is the differences that sharpen or give vitality to the commonalities, it would seem that the necessity of a culture to accept and respond to such diversities is a requisite to creative production.

Many pages could be written concerning art and its relative importance from a cultural standpoint. It can be briefly stated, however, that the control of this cultural empire is ninety-nine and one-hundred percent from the white group. This is not because whites are more "cultured" but because they control the economy and consequently dictate the specific aesthetic standards. This condition will persist so long as we continue to follow the prevailing archaic, computerized style of aesthetics insisted upon by those in command. It is without question that the present operations of the "world of art" function in the manner of a closed society.

It is long past time for us to fully realize that artists are really different from each other—just as people are different from each other. One might venture to say that artists are people.

There are artists and men of science of varying capabilities in all cultures. In this book we lay no claim that a man's ethnic origin makes him better or worse. It is felt that a man's ethnic origin gives him license to be different in matters related to creativeness.

BLACK ARTISTS ON ART presents the work of some of the many individuals who deserve to be called artist. They are individuals of varying degrees of interests and abilities. They are individuals who have continued as active producing artists in spite of the many obstacles that confront all artists. Many of the artists featured in BLACK ARTISTS ON ART are as yet unrecognized as artists. They have, however, through art found a means of expression which confirms them as individuals.

BLACK ARTISTS ON ART is a book to promote change—change in order that art might function as expression rather than as an institution. It could open many doors and many minds for it is varied enough in its orientation to serve as a point of departure for many avenues of expression.

This book is not limited to the area of art but rather it could easily be considered as a vital contribution to comparative studies. BLACK ARTISTS ON ART is not intended to be a book with answers but one with ideas—ideas that could serve to stimulate men's minds in order that they might broaden their scope and thereby reflect in a "timeless" sense the differences in orientation of a truly creative society.

Samella S. Lewis

Art critics are going to have to expand their minds and concepts in order to evaluate this publication in its entirety. True, a line is still a line and composition is still composition but there are different kinds of lines and compositions, and these kinds are going to continue and grow whether or no.

Art is not an intellectual exercise, approached through structured learning, emotions, styles, and practised in museums, galleries, and private "collections." Art is spiritual, the primary function of which is for the benefit, growth and improvement of the human animal. The artists and craftsmen were left out of the social revolution that attended the industrial revolution. Today we are on the threshold of another revolution: technocracy, computation. The social revolution which will attend it leaves us no choice but to undergo deep, psychological change in our instinctive attitudes toward the world and its peoples.

Artists and craftsmen will lead the way and the black artist will be at the head of the procession because he has never been permitted substitution of "things" for human values. From whatever point of view, aesthetic or social, he has always had to tell it "like it is."

Ruth G. Waddy

CONTENTS

CONTENTS

lucille d. roberts

EMERGENCE, 40"x48"

. . . Commenting on a painting that portrays African nations emerging from the past into independence is Newton Ifedayo Miller-Aganyemi, a first-year student at the D. C. Teachers College (right). Artist Lucille Roberts (left) and Dr. Matthew Whitehead, Dean of the college, join in the discussion. In the foreground are visitors to the gallery.

BLACK IS BEAUTIFUL, 24"x48"

. . . Gripped by the concept of Negritude both in the African milieu
and here in the United States, I cannot, after much soul searching,
accept for myself as a black artist, the path of impersonal,
purely intellectual expression. I must affirm the identity, dignity and
beauty of the black man.

gary a. rickson

. . . Truth and the reality of truth is always in constant study.
This study is for me a science that relates to my art and to me . . .
a confirmation of my emotional existence.

. . . The mural, done in what I call black expressionist technique,
is there to counteract the lack of black art in the Museum of Fine Arts
in Boston. But also to create an out-door museum of functional art,
as the mural is a backdrop   for a playground, which is now used
by the area's children.

(Dana Chandler worked the mural's lower half; more of his work may
be seen, starting on page 39.)

arthur carraway

. . . In order to really develop as a painter one must explore the direction physically. My idea was to experiment in painting through African forms. This meant going to Africa, the mother of all development.

AFRICAN SYMBOL OF WISDOM   oil, 34"x38"

ACROSS THE HUDSON, oil

FETISH FORM, Series II, 1968, oil, 36"x50"   FETISH FORM, oil

6

phillip lindsay mason

. . . My work is concerned with universal equivalents:
the social phenomena of life on earth. Black life.
Images. Black images. Dream images.
My work is concerned with the calling of one's bluff with one's self.
Nitty gritty. Bugaloo.
And outer space too.
My work is concerned with what black people have been.
What they are now. And what they could be.
My work is concerned with the blues
                  and paying dues.
My work is concerned with the cliche and the
unknown for life is both a mixture of the cliche
and the unknown.
My work is concerned with me doing my thing.
Growing
Sowing
       my seeds
producing flowers/weeds
in the soil of this land.
My work is concerned with "the man"
No! Not that man!
Black, beautiful (enigmatic) man.
My work is concerned with loud colors, new rhythms
New/old things.
Circles, rings.
My work is concerned with how we love
how we lie
how we smile
how we cry
how we move
          be still
          until . . .
See?
My work is concerned with
Me.

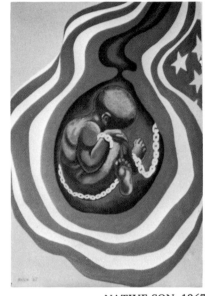

NATIVE SON, 1967

ODETTA, 1967

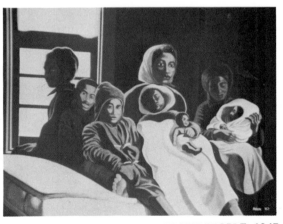

BLUES PEOPLE, 1967

Lithograph, Zebra Series

margo humphrey

. . . Art, to me, is a relationship of symbols
which formulate an idea, bringing into being thoughts of the past and present
in a contemporary way which relates to my environment.

Lithograph, Zebra Series

Lithograph, Zebra Series

SOME FIELDS HAVE MORE
FLOWERS THAN GRASS,
Lithograph

I'M NOT REALLY LISTENING,
Lithograph

THE NEW GARDEN, oil, 26"x30"

SOCIAL READJUSTMENT, oil, 4'x6'

raymond howell

FROM A GREAT PAST, 24"x38"

I was in Africa two years through the auspices of the United Nations.
Though I traveled through the West, North and South of Africa, I spent one year
in East Africa—Dar es Salaam, Tanganyika (now Tanzania) and Mombasa,
Kenya. It was there that I became acquainted with Makonde sculpture by touring
the museums and art shops. Their work was most impressive. Through the
Makonde sculpture different forms and ideas began to take shape in my mind
toward a new and positive approach to painting that is related to my own cultural
direction and development. The direction is not yet clearly defined, but then is
any art form clearly defined or understood in the period in which it is painted?

THE BROWN PAINTING
oil, 4'x6'

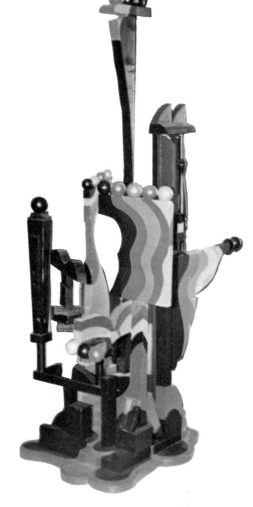

ibibio fundi

. . . Until this year, I have purposely avoided any statement about my work. This silence was brought about by my great distaste for the stock collection of words used by Western academia to analyze art.

If one knew how to conjugate the verb "to be" and remembered the magic words: form, color, line, personal imagery, etc., etc., etc., one could construct enough esoteric sentences about art to delight the most exacting professor. I loathed these periods of prescribed intellectual analysis.

I wanted to do, to see, to feel, to be, to act, to work. And if I did speak about my art, I wanted the words to be natural and unaffected—spontaneous and not contrived. I wanted to speak in the language of my black peers, but the intellectuals (or pseudo-intellectuals) who dominated the art scene would have this unacceptable.

Because of this conflict, I left the University and created my own world of phantasy. My work itself became my only statement, a silent parody on Western man's most prized possession, the machine.

I am speaking now because of my involvement with New Perspectives in Black Art, an exhibit in Oakland, California. At this show, there were no esoteric speeches about POP, OP, FUNK or MYSTIC ART. There were no formal dogmas about form, line, color, and imagery. Instead, these artists spoke about their works with great simplicity, spontaneity and compassion. They also spoke of their dual roles—social activists and cultural leaders of this 20th Century Black Renaissance, this revolutionary re-birth of joy and self affirmation.

It is good to be a small part of this Great New Breed—a breed united in its efforts to replace the black man's hopelessness, frustration and despair with new hope, new pride and dignity.

I can speak now because all of this is meaningful to me. Art and life can never be divorced. Ask any black artist. Ask me.

14

NON-KINETIC MOTOR

for The Good Ship Lollipop

WOODEN SKETCH
for Possible Non-Functioning Machine   16

laura w. williams

FIGURE, oil, 47"x15"

. . . As a painter of abstract paintings, I do not usually begin with anything so concrete as a preconception. At some point in its loose development, the canvas seems to dictate to me and I proceed under this influence until I sense that it is time to stop. This involves my "getting lost" under the persuasion of forms and color to such an extent that I often wonder, in looking at the finished painting, that "I" did it.

UNTITLED

RED FIGURE, oil

18

john t. harris

. . . I paint portraits and illustrations.
I like to work in watercolor, oil or
carbon pencil. I enjoy working
with all kinds of racial types, old
and young.

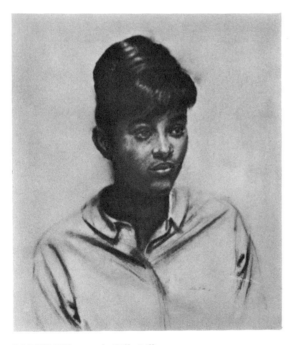

PORTRAIT, pastel, 18"x24"

PORTRAIT, oil, 16"x20"

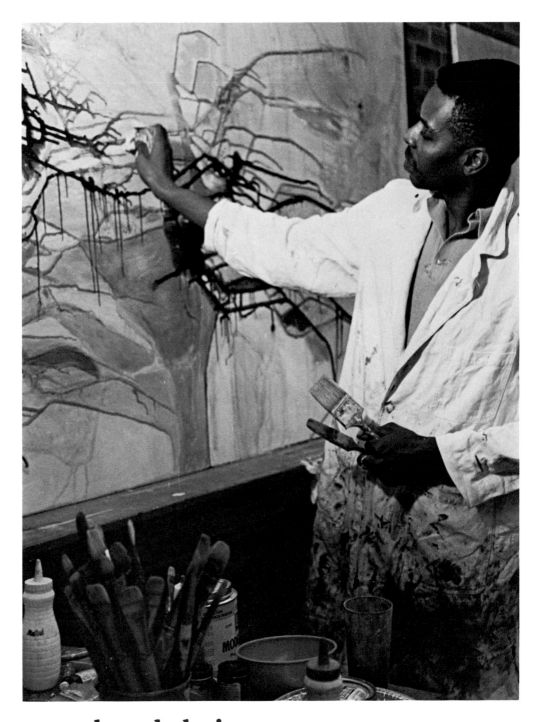

arthur l. britt sr.

. . . Art to me is data gathered and recorded of events, expressed in my own individual way. This, I believe, is the way it should be: "A Record of Time kept through painting." The medium I use is paint, no matter what kind; if it can be used for the job, then it is good.

Don't worry about others because most of the time other people cannot understand anyway, so why worry? I work for myself and express myself the very best that I can at each given time.

SWAMP, mixed media, 36"x40"

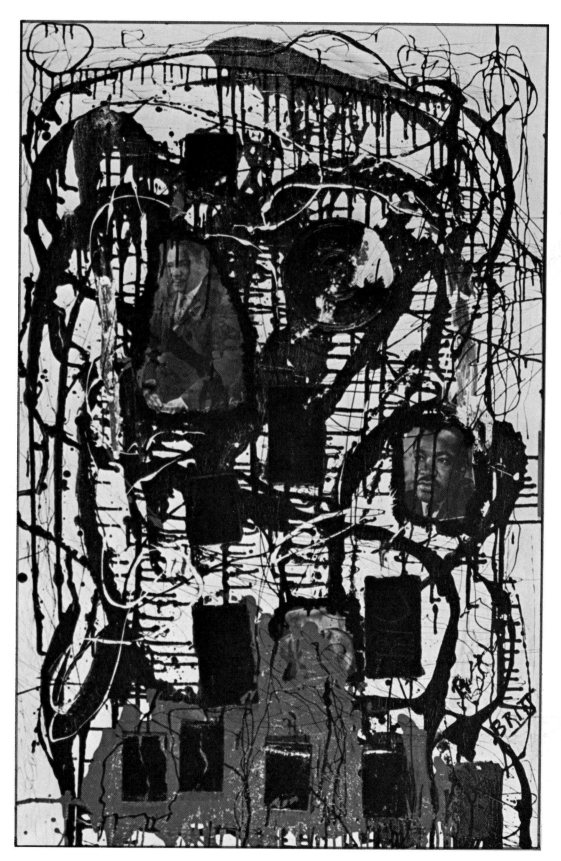

THE DREAM, mixed media

. . . I consider myself to be a graphic impressionist and I strive for synthesis of expression in both figurative and non-figurative work.

For the black artist, the drastic social and political charges motivated by Civil Rights movements and legislation have given him a new awareness and has made America conscious of his presence and involvement in the contemporary art scene, in many respects, similar to how the New Deal Era affected American artists of that period. Finally, the black artist, en masse, is on the active art scene!

robert raleigh d'hue jr.

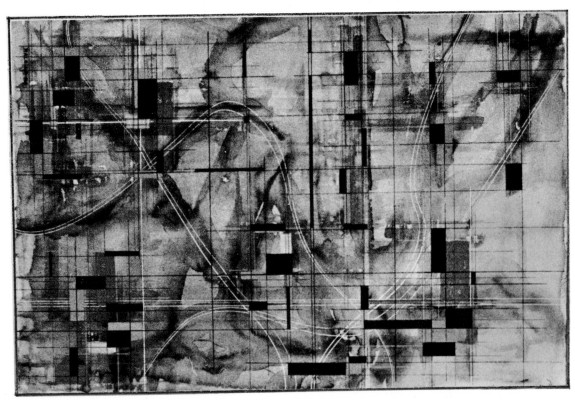

HAZE

john wilfred outterbridge

. . . I paint, draw and carve not beauty, for beauty you can see all around you, and it is forever made so obvious as in super department stores and other such places. But I rather like the effort to understand the ordinary things, people and places that stand close by, not readily seen by many and seldom heard. Get to know these things, for they are complete and very much a part of us. Then go beyond that which is normally referred to as beauty.

Presently my professor is love and life, my school is dedication to truth of expression. I am deeply involved with humanity and much less sacred subjects in an attempt to create an art that is a kind of deity. I work hard because I care hard, with the hope of someday becoming a total artist.

MOGO GHETTO, wood, 2½'x3'

RECLINING FIGURE, wood-metal, 4'x4'x3'

BIRTH PROCESS, wood-metal, 1'x2'

25

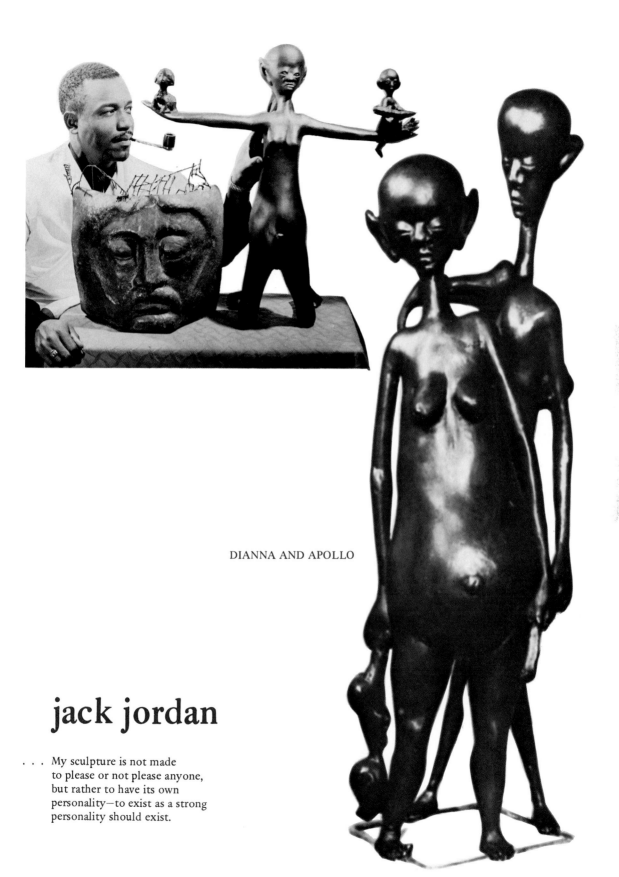

DIANNA AND APOLLO

jack jordan

. . . My sculpture is not made
to please or not please anyone,
but rather to have its own
personality—to exist as a strong
personality should exist.

26

arthur berry

. . . As an artist, I ascribe to no single school or credo. I work with several media trying always to address myself to the world around me. In my work, I attempt to deal with the problems which man meets as man. I strive to make him more sensitive to himself as an individual—an individual feeling and comprehending his environment while coming to know that environment and himself intimately. This sensitivity depends upon the kind of people and environment we finally make of ourselves and our world.

Unfinished Figure, 18"

BANG! ABEL, 1966, acrylic-collage, 34"x48"

phillip j. hampton

I am attracted by the Gestalt of our time.
In this generation, I am concerned about the
complexity of people, things, materials and ideas.
(I am even concerned about the why of a tiny bud.)
All of them seek expression that is, finally,
a whole rather than a confounding of parts.
I expect, indeed, I anticipate that a new form
will emerge—quietly, perhaps mystically.
Maybe its form, in its purest sense, will not
be embraced as an art entity. Nonetheless, it will
have had its insemination and gestation in the
seething studios of the artists.

Therefore, I am interested to know the
techniques and attitudes of old masters, and practice
the seek-and-discovery technique with materials
and ideas that I have brought to my studio.
Nothing can happen for me without thought
and contemplation. I admire the Ife and the
ancient T'ang artist for this trait. I want my
studio to contribute to the birth of the new order.
Nevertheless, I know well that in our generation, no
one artist will bring forth the one NEW order.
In our time genius is reflected as the work of
many. I try to discover and contribute.

fred brown

. . . The 20th Century black artist apart from his own striving for esthetic perfection is responsible to the black people who populate the world. The black artist cannot remain content with the expression of "pure art" at the expense of his socio-political labors, particularly in the area of subject matter.

UNTITLED

roland welton

UNTITLED

. . . Ready or not I am here, accept me. Art is beautiful just like black and white and all the colors. And it is everywhere—you cannot deny it. I wish I had more time to study it as a human being—not in a hateful atmosphere. When I was a child my parents and teachers knew that art was everywhere and they tried to guide me into that knowledge but they were unable to find a means of communicating.

I have wandered around the world. When at last I came to New York and decided to study art, I realized then that many people in the past had tried to guide me. During the time I traveled, I found many kinds of hate, but with art I found that I could have love in my individual world. As I walk through the looking glass, I see visions of all kinds of shapes and forms which only I can make into a beautiful world for me.

Others may enjoy shapes and colors that for me are frustration. So I am challenging the world—a better communication between me and you and you and you and you. Ready or not here I am, accept me.

UNTITLED

. . . A pneumatic ordinance inside me thinks. It gets slowed down when I drive to keep time. It will not do, but feels—you can't stop it, you hi-jack it in space, painting; if you can hold on.

My father is railroad poor and hip—looks black exactly different, influenced me. He brought me his train when I couldn't speak—backing thru school. He was my resistance. Others, here are Shakespeare, Coltrane, Garvey, Kierkegaard, Christ, Freud, N. Turner, Spinoza, weather, topography, night and women.

In term, twentieth century paint; the cubist-solipsists at the African wheel, clean paperdolls, unnecessarily. In prostitution the satisfaction is clerical, or Pop art, Op (still life in general) and other numb feasts are back there too—getting paid for it now, with that artificial sweetener, "blowup." Jackson Pollock has held. He loved jazz and the ground. He evaporates the dance but music evokes intact. When he opened a door it came off. To use the field he had to miss the snow. He said you can't judge a book by its cover. The dominant art movements have backed up ever since (note contemporary psychedelic nouveau), as the revolution advances, in this here Reconstruction Era.

lawrence mc gaugh

SLEEPING MAN, 30"x40"

31

LEAPING FIGURES, 17"x14"

elaine towns

. . . In my paintings and drawings, I hope others can recognize and enjoy my revelations about people, things and life. I want to share those things that are important to me, not merely to record, but to present ideas to which people can respond. I want to give the work all the love and care I feel, hoping that others will be touched.

michael kavanaugh perry

Being a painter, sculpture is not important; what one does, is doing—IMPORTANT.

WALKING, STANDING, WALKING, 1968, intaglio

34

betye saar

. . . I have been involved with the mystic image for some time. In my search to produce a graphic sensation, I have used my prints or portions of prints combined them with drawings, and framed them in windows with many small panes. The window is a symbolic structure which allows the viewer to look into it to gain insight and to traverse the threshold of the mystic world.

My graphic interpretation is to create an occult atmosphere which will leave a strong impression of the vague and unexplained in the mind of the viewer and to give his imagination free rein to explore the mystery of human destiny, of change, of fate and of the quest of knowledge of the future.

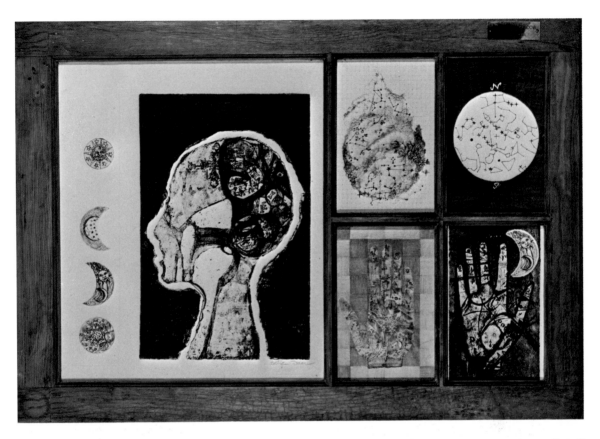

THE MYSTIC WINDOW, intaglio and drawing, 20"x30"

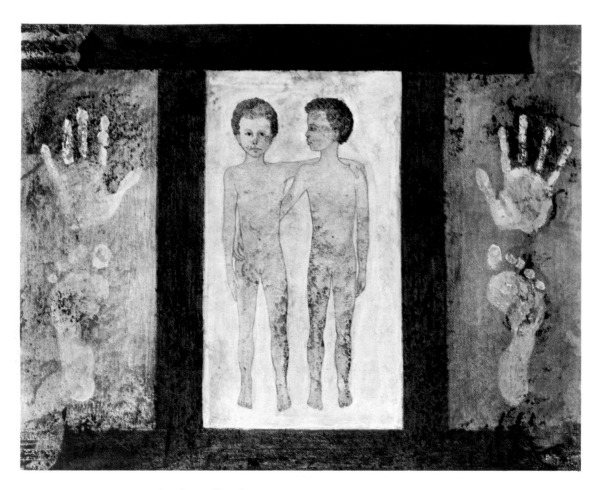

THE JEWEL OF GEMINI, drawing, 18"x23"

BUST

annette lewis ensley

. . . Art embraces the hand of man, yields and reflects his innate talent; without once checking to see what color the hand may be. Thank God. My art is privately me flowing out to meet public interpretation.

henry brownlee

. . . The black art of the ghetto should be classified with the masters of the 15th and 16th Centuries, and yet in this age of atomic and electronic automation, the black man's art has not been discovered. I remember the time of my earliest days in the ghetto on the West Side of Savannah, scratching in the wet sand in front of my slum house after a rainy summer day with several other neighborhood friends, expressing a talent that I was not myself aware of, nor were my friends.

The black man in America has a rich culture to give to his native land—America . . . the black man in the ghetto has a great reward for his land that he loves—the culture and art of a brave black people, for we are a beautiful people.

THREE BLACK SISTERS

dana c. chandler jr.

. . . I am a black artist whose work is directed expressly toward the education of blacks as to their true position of oppression in a White Racist Society, and to the development of a new third world concept in black art. We must develop our standards concerning black art and move away from past identification with, and adherence to, castrating white standards. Black art is a tremendous force for education and political development which we have ignored. I mean to tell it like it is. I "ain't" subtle and I don't intend to become subtle so long as America remains the great white destroyer.

As to my style, it's black expressionism, done in vivid colors, raw, earthy, much use of Day-glo. If the system does not destroy me, I will move into plastics and do with plastic sculpture what I've done in acrylics and tempera. I use all kinds of surfaces, whatever I can get my hands on. Obviously, I do not make a great deal of money with my works; in fact, my works have been defaced and destroyed, 11 major pieces at last count. But I will not stop painting . . . only death can stop me, as it does everyone.

Peace and Black Power, Brothers and Sisters.

A major work, which depicts Uncle Sam
with his foot on a Black man's head.
Also, the foot print shows how our strivings
are surpressed. The path is blood . . .

LAND OF THE FREE, 1967

We are imprisoned by American Democracy;
democratic principles do apply to us. And
now that we've discovered that black is
beautiful, and all civilization comes from us,
we can expect greater repression.

LAND OF THE FREE #2

We are not free!
The constant persecution
of all our heroes proves
this! We are still being
lynched, raped, brutalized,
and I'm not going
to let us forget it. Sure,
we've made progress,
but only that which
we've died for.

NIGGER . . . YOU ARE A
FOUR HUNDRED YEAR PRISONER!

Showing LeRoi Jones in jail, America's way of dealing with blackness. The colors of the flag are red, yellow, and blue, for the cowardly way that America deals with black heroes.

We blacks love our heroes and will choose our own. The brothers who did their thing at the Olympics were beautiful and got the hero's welcome from fellow blacks that they deserved when they got home.

LE ROI JONES—HOUSE ARREST

My way of saying that the old stereotyped Uncle Tom is dying. We will fight violently, if necessary, for all that is owed us by right of birth. Black is beautiful.

DEATH OF UNCLE TOM, 1968

My way of saying that black is beautiful. This work tells the pride of black America in its own power and genius, and is an example of my belief that black Americans who survive to the age of twenty-one, still retain their manhood and pride must be geniuses, since America tries so desperately to destroy all our heroes and all our men.

MOSES BRINGS THE WORD
TO HIS PEOPLE, 1967

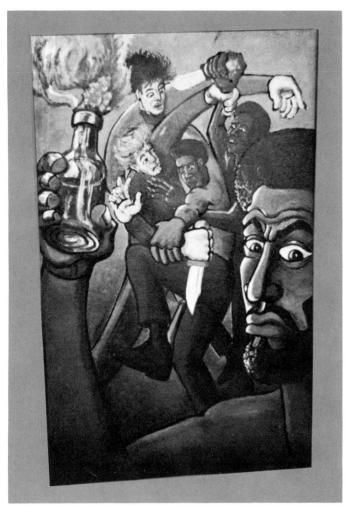

REBELLION '68

. . . It's my belief that more of this kind of
confrontation will happen during the next
decade. Things will get very bloody.

42

jene ballentine

Thinking about art
Thoughts of artistic statements
Through the mind of mine I see
Images of black and white with color
Color with black and white
Real sharp
Sharper than real
Sharper than real
Non-cutting if protected,
Protection not required
To see what is meant by me
Hoping to mean more than
Can be seen by me or you
Painting what I say, the painting is the
Statement, I am only the interpreter
In to oil. Oil not necessary
To mean what I say but to
Say in any medium is necessary.
Upon the handle of my brush
I am riding colors of impact,
Colors of the spectrum of
Life. I ride swiftly in order
Not to forget the
Route to the root. The root
Not yet obtained.

Nirvana no doubt.

BORN FREE, 1968

HAD I BEEN BOLD OR SLIGHTLY BRAVE, 1967

bernie casey

. . . My paintings approach surrealism but they are not as severe. They are concepts, thoughts, remembered experiences, and things like that.

Art in itself can sometimes be completely terrifying. Many times the insight with which an artist looks at the world is so telling and all inclusive that the mind boggles. I am pretentious enough to believe that I have something to say, and bold enough to say it! The underlying reason being that if I couldn't, I would surely die. And death is forever.

SCHIZOPHRENIC MOON FOLLY, 1968

. . . Black art to me must be vibrant and alive, it must reflect love, sacrifice and anger. I have no great philosophical messages to pass on in my paintings, although I believe that each person is a philosopher according to the way that he or she is shaped and molded by his or her environment and his or her experiences in life. I paint for pleasure. Pleasure for me and what pleases me may perhaps please other people when they look at it.

kitty l. hayden

PINK LANDSCAPE

BLUE LANDSCAPE

DESIGN

angela l. perkins

In order to communicate well, one must have a good command of the language. Meaningful communication comes for the artist when he knows and understands his society—its loves,and hates, its rights and wrongs, its needs and aspirations. The combination of imagination, awareness, and skill is the language of an artist—a communicator.

49

. . . In a world of confusion where eternal hope for the innocent is unstable, where parents have neglected to teach the principles of God's law, and the want for money has outweighed the purity and innocence of upbringing, I think this is the root of society's downfall.

The young human interest in contrasting colors of a confused and combustible world, starts before adolescence. There and then purity is challenged.

The church in view symbolizes confusion; it is of the world, it is constructed by man. "God dwelleth not in temples made by hands." Acts 17:24-25. As for religious institutions, politics is becoming the Sunday message, again the challenge. Pure in heart is the innocent remaining innocent. That is God's law, not man's.

william reid

. . . For a long, long time, I have been obsessed with a desire to master the potter's craft. There has never been enough time, nor has it been possible to abandon all else in the pursuit of excellence in this direction. In spite of this, there is an occasional sense of excitement followed by a warming serenity that occurs when the clay is particularly responsive to my touch. More and more time is devoted to the challenges of form and texture, and thus, the pursuit of perfection continues . . .

della brown taylor

STONEWARE VASE, hand-built slab construction

51

COUNTY SEAT

. . . I believe that the expressionist
artist has a function to create simply,
but with a vibrant force, a pictorial
scene of man and his surroundings.
The craftsman with his hands,
but the artist with his heart.

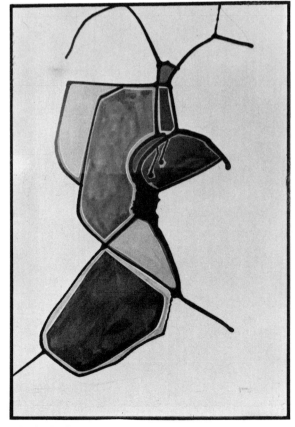

donald o. greene

ANTELERS

52

amos white

. . . It is my aim to create
works of art which
satisfy the needs of
aesthetically-sentient
persons who wish to
surround themselves
with objects that
reflect their own
individuality.

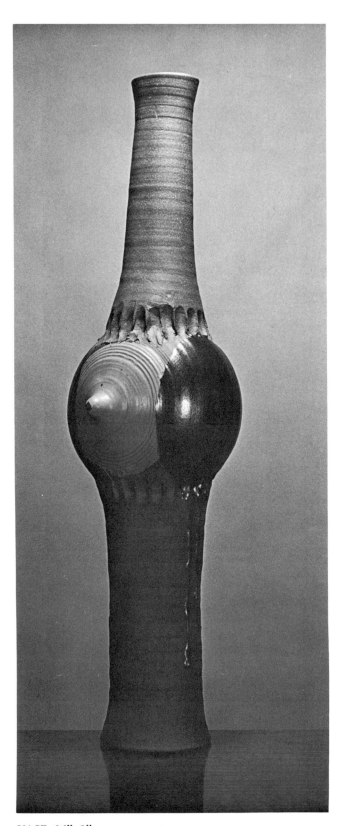

VASE, 36"x9"

STONEWARE VASE

. . . My art reflects the frustrations and anxieties inherent in being black today. But concurrently with my social content, I strive to create art of uniquely integrated forms, attempting to involve the viewer in his dual vision of personal and aesthetic awareness. Art must allow room for the human element to come through, yet the artist must have an understanding of his craft, plus an awareness of forms to bring substance to the art object.

ben hazard

SELF PORTRAIT, acrylic

BIRD WITH DEAD MATE, acrylic

l. compton kolawole

. . . Tradition blossoms in a multitude of customs but basically it is only one thing:
the philosophical backbone of a people or race to answer its disposition on earth.
Our tradition, the philosophical answer of Africa, is very different from other traditions
and very similar to the philosophy of nature. In the basic motive of my art I try to
make this philosophy—nature's invisible reality—visible with transforming its image
into imagery. THE INVISIBLE HAS NO IMAGERY. Neither transforming it into symbols.
Most of all it expresses the unity of space and time. . . .

It has been said that African art did to the artists of this century what the antique did
to the Renaissance people. I cannot agree . . . that modern European art is a result
of this confrontation . . . the artist . . . projected the big adventure of scientific technique . . .
pattern, structure and regulation—order of inside matter. And in spite of poetic programs
. . . the less it satisfied spiritually, the more recognition it received as if to force the human
well-being away from a . . . due revolution of human behavior.

The art revolution has been started by Afro-American musicians and dancers; I myself
carry it over into paintings.

THREE FOR DAVIS, oil

CONSTRUCTION, 1968, mixed media, 36"

marie e. johnson

. . . In a country where human values are constantly being raped and murdered in the name of technological and economic progress, black art must deal with the common humanity which unites all mankind.

Black art's function is the rediscovery of its own roots, and the examining of the depths of the beauty, poignancy, and the humor in the souls of black people. We are a people who protest, pray, curse and preach, sing, moan, grunt and scream, laugh, cry, live and love. I am to produce a portrait of a people: the reservoir of images is unlimited.

CONSTRUCTION

CONSTRUCTION, mixed media, 60"

CONSTRUCTION, mixed media

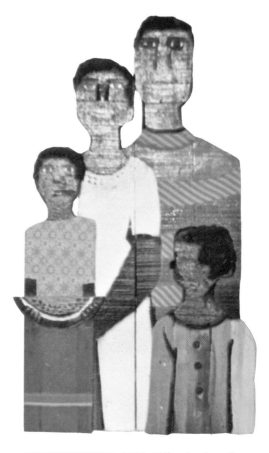

CONSTRUCTION, 1968, 22", mixed media

DARK REFUGE, 48"x36"

CONSTRUCTION, 1968, mixed media, 22"

60

william mc neil

. . . America is racked by tensions, suffering and fears of the deepest proportions. It remains economically the first nation, but it sadly lacks an abiding sense of love. If, however the humanist could delve into this malady, and be given a chance to inform this condition with profound art, the spirit of the country could be regained, or gained. I take a strong and earnest stand on this matter, which concerns me deeply. People are my main concern; their environment, the seasons of their lives and the sufferings of the heart.

. . . The black artist needs much more recognition than he is presently getting: his work should be seen in a wide variety of places, and more books should be written about him. Too many people have not known enough about the diverse accomplishments of blacks. Some very fine work is being done, and more people should become acquainted with the fact that there is talent in many fields in black communities.

doris crudup

SOUL MAN

robert h. green jr.

. . . Art presents itself to man through every area of society and nature, and the artist expresses as he feels. Lately, I have become interested in letting the line express visual and invisible things as well as sound. Color is part of the expression but the line is more dominate. My thesis on "Emotional Factor of Selected Musical Compositions" revealed what I have attempted to do with the intangible which is to be felt, not seen—art expressed by linear movements.

THERE IS NO GREATER LOVE

FLOWER POT, 16"x20"

FRIENDS, oil, 20"x24"

brenda rogers

Faces of happiness, despair, faces of
re-stimulated black manhood . . . these
seem to consume my canvas wearing
expressions with which we can identify.
Possibly my main objective in painting
is that it gives us an opportunity to
look at ourselves and really understand
that we are beautiful.

Untitled, 1968, oil

CHILD, 1964, oil

The human condition is my primary
interest in art. I try to interpret life
around me by using a few tubes of color,
brushes, charcoal, zinc plate and so
forth—any media that can express what
I want to say.

charles d. rogers

. . . Painting is Joy to me: it allows me to give
expressions of inner thoughts, emotions,
through creative activity from a keen awareness
of my environment.

mary parks washington

HOPE, CONSTRUCTION, mixed media

leon n. hicks

. . . It is evident that the art of the minority group artist indicates that the physical appearance of his pictorial surface(s) are the pre-eminent concerns of his art. The materials of his art possess for him an immediacy, and they supply him with the means of acquiring in his art the urgent socio-value and need-fulfillment that an embodiment of art provides him.

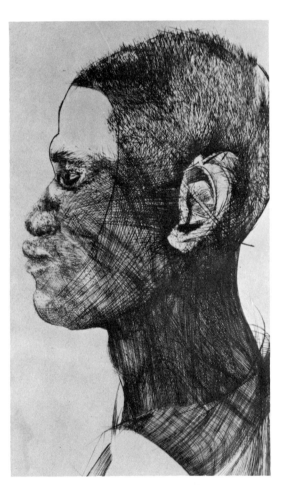

BLACK BOY, 1961, intaglio, 10"x18"

APOGEE, 1962, intaglio, 30"x40"

APPALACHIAN SEQUELA #6, 1967, intaglio, 18"x24"

david mann

. . . All art is the distillation of the sensory perception and reception of the human senses: taste, touch, sound and sight. Whether it be music, sculpture, painting, writing, architecture, photography, dancing, and so forth. As brevity is the soul of wit, so too is simplicity the essence of art.

Ultimately, in whatever medium that the artist chooses to express himself, the criteria by which his work is measured depends upon the care and concern for the medium. Care for the idea he is trying to express and concern for the finished product—be it a sonnet, sonata, painting, building, or a relationship with his fellow man.

COLLARDS, watercolor, 15"x20"

william paja

... Art is a means of telling the many and varied stories of my people—their problems, tragedies, hopes, dreams, aspirations and yes, even their weaknesses—the aesthetics of which are almost incidental.

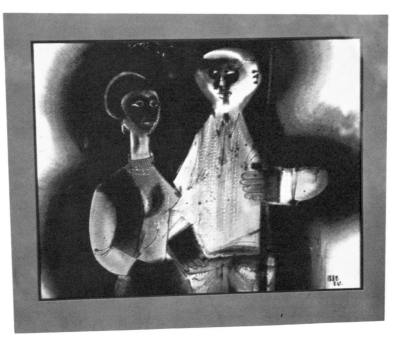

HUSTLIN' THE HUSTLER, watercolor, 15"x20"

THE WAGES OF SIN IS BREAD, watercolor, 22"x28"

103rd STREET POULTRY MARKET, watercolor, 22"x28"

YES, LEROI, oil

david p. bradford

. . . Just as jazz evolved out of black people in America, so shall black art. It is a difficult task to be sure, because we as black artists must unlearn all that we have been taught that art should be, and at the same time maintain very high standards for black art.

By a black art, I do not mean a painting of a black woman with a rag on her head. A black art must have the rhythm, freedom and excitement of a John Coltrane solo as well as make a statement to its viewer. Also black art must be folksy and natural. By this I mean it must derive from pure talent and not from the arrangement of light bulbs and tin foil; for the experiences of black people in America have been a folksy experience and black people the world over are close to nature and the natural process of things in nature.

I think the times we live in now demand that the black artist produce what the Mexicans call "popular" art. That is, we must make statements to and for black people. It is foolish for black artists to think in terms of "art for art's sake," for the experiences of black people (and any art produced by black people must derive from black experience) in America has been and continues to be a struggle against racism, injustice and induced cultural defecation.

Only when we omit the desire to make it in the white man's art world, only when we omit the desire to place the making of money first with our art, can we produce a popular art, a black art, an art that speaks to and for black people. Until we as black artists realize these things, we shall continue to lay in the dark of the white man's shadow.

I hope my work evolves to the things I have just spoken of. I am experimenting with double images at this point in my work, that I may state a problem and at the same time give the problem a solution. I am also experimenting with collages in my drawings and paintings. I want to show the inner beauty and strength of black Americans and glorify those black people who have contributed so much to our people.

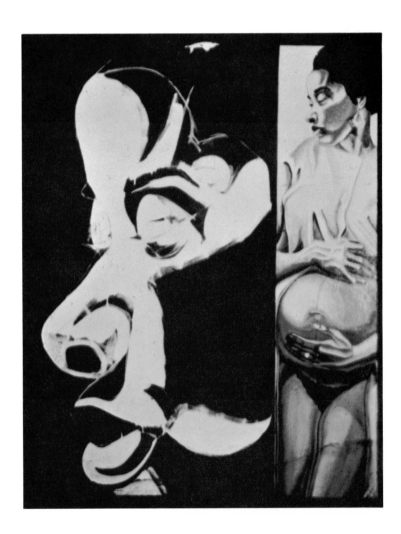

royce h. vaughn

. . . Art is not a capital "A" subject. Art, in my opinion, is primarily an experience in honesty. The experience is prime, the result may or may not be important to the artist or others who wish to judge it.

It is my deepest belief that the artist's most important function is to translate the totality of life's experience and perception. As translator, he should be sensible in communicating with means and imagination and manner that are as relevant as they are necessary.

The one thing the world and the artist do not need is rationalism without reason, reality or direction. If one must insist on assigning "style" or my work, it pleases me to call it personal impressionism on a scientific experimental axis.

GLAD RAGS, collage, 46"x37"

THE BOYS, collage, 46"x36"

MALCOLM SPOKE, oil, 38"x48"

73

UNTITLED, oil

larry walker

. . . A major aspect of my creative pursuits seems to be my concern for the relationship
of shapes to their existing environment. Often these shapes appear as human images,
sometimes as enigmatic forces that suggest natural phenomena. The dominating
factor which seems to bind these aspects has been the evolvement of a circular picture
plane and a competition stripe. For me, both of these elements seem to have
philosophical overtones. I view the circles as an environment in which symbolic form
moves and exists—often suppressed by the outer shell, doomed to a life cycle of
introversion. On occasion the imagery demonstrates adequate force and determination
to release itself from its environmental womb—as a fully developed fetus emerges to
another kind of existence—as a student graduates and leaves the protective umbrella
of one environment for that of another—as a volcano regurgitates its interior to the
surface of the earth. Often the imagery appears as mankind, alienated, defeated,
rejected or disillusioned, his spirit hampered by an ever-present competition barrier.
Yet, there are indications of hope, possibilities for man to still find ways to actively
participate in the real meaning of life. I find that in pursuit of these concerns, the
work poses many challenges and the process of involvement continues to generate a
multiplicity of forms and ideas which are combining with my training and aesthetic
awareness and pressing for direct expression.

CHILDREN OF SOCIETY 14
charcoal and conté
24"x28"

CHILDREN OF SOCIETY 17
charcoal and conté
29"x29"

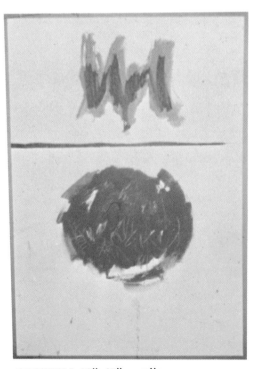

GROWTH I, 29"x37", acrylic

MICROSCAPE I
watercolor, 19½"x12½"

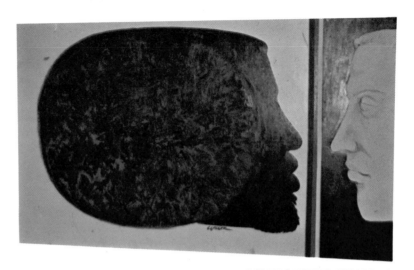

MY THOUGHTS, MY IDEAS

UNTITLED, oil, 36"x40"

THREE WOMEN, 1968, oil, 30"x40"

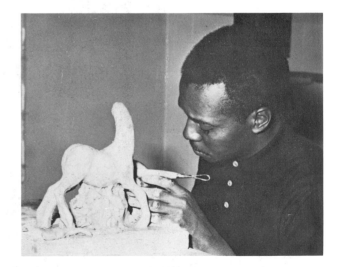

bernard wright

. . . As an artist I would like my work to speak for itself. In these paintings I am trying to show strength, not only of body, but of mind as well. Without these you do not survive as a person, a nation or as a people. We have endured . . . we shall survive!

FERTILITY, oil, 18"x24"

eugene grigsby

. . . The young black American artist is accepting the challenge of his African heritage. For decades, the black artists have been cognizant of this heritage and its challenge, and they have done as much as any group to stress the meanings of this heritage. Only recently, however, has the sense of this message broken through to the general public. This message gains power and fuller meaning in the works of these young artists.

william maxwell

. . . The extent of my involvement with life . . . my social, economic, domestic, and ethnic background are the major influencing factors of my work. My ethnic background is probably the greatest and most important influencing factor because it is from that base which ideas originate and perspectives are molded.

TEXTURE—LA CORRIDA, mixed media, 48"x54"

JOMO #1, ceramic, 14"

raymond lark

. . . My goal is to promote artists, both young and old, who combine ability with desire to work hard. While hoping to encourage and stimulate other artists, I also wish to further the appreciation and understanding of the arts as they relate to the development of the American artist. My work speaks for itself.

SWEET PEACHES, 1968, graphite

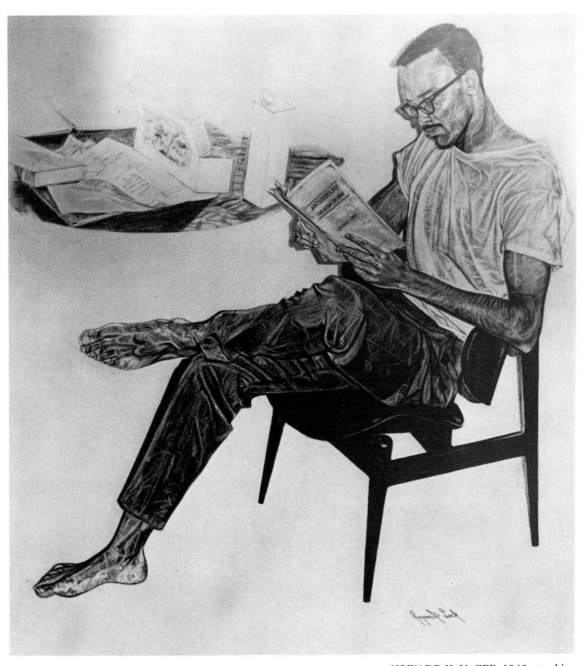

HOWARD H. McGEE, 1968, graphite

wes hall

. . . I became an artist because of my great desire to magnify life in a visual way that stabs below the surface of beautiful objects and exposes their real inner beauty. I've tried to illustrate in such a zoom-in and camera revealing manner that mere eyebrows, upper lips, and the joy of an actor's triumphant yell is matched by only the beauty of a bitten, delicious apple, a fine piece of graphics, or a giant redwood tree exposing a fawn hovering near it for the protection of a home. I am an artist because I feel great imaginations of creativity can be said visually in an illustrated manner without any editing to reduce its true magnitude.

Art is a love, it is where I need never dream. All systems are "go" when Art and I are joined as a team. There are no BLACKS or WHITES or PURPLES that have predominance in my world of art. I just sing through my hands, having and hoping, but not caring that there will be choirs of viewers to see the production, with honesty being the supporting cast.

AWARENESS

MONUMENTAL MAN, 1968, oil, 5'x6'

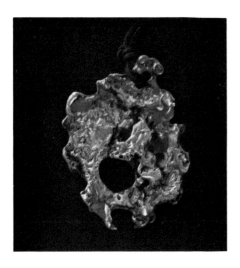

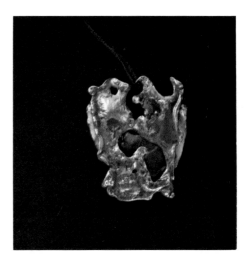

. . . As artists say: I am doing my thing in metals and enameling, with other crafts and photography running a hot second.

In order to work these two materials successfully, I found I would have to explore almost every art form and media. In today's art often one has to combine many materials for the piece to take on the shape, color, and excitement one wishes the viewer to experience. My inspiration comes from nature first and second from the twisted rubble and discarded forms left by man against the beautiful forms of nature. Whenever possible, I use materials in the state they are found. Whatever the media, the surface of my work must have a textured or shaped surface. I prefer to create art that is functional rather than art that is only decorative.

evangeline j. montgomery

james dallas parks

. . . I am very much influenced
by my friend, Thomas Hart Benton
and interested in painting the Negro scene.

VIEW OVER MONTERREY, MEXICO, 1959, watercolor

donald e. coles

. . . Lately, pure observation has opened up activities in nature that seem new to my vision. Energy is that force that thrusts a wave off the sea surging upward. The mound of clear ocean water weighing tons lifts before our eyes and dashes itself against the rock shore. The shattering weight perpetually recoils with all its velocity in its undercurrents. To line is to see this energy in the vitality of matter and movement and to experience the same pulsating motion within.

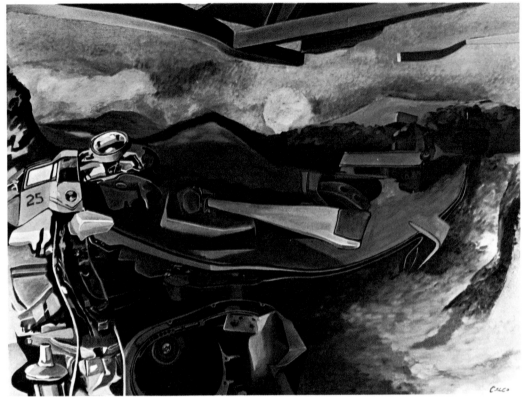

UNTITLED, oil

UNTITLED, oil

89

BOATS AT DEAL ISLAND, acrylic, 34"x10"

jimmie mosely

. . . The things I see, the people
I meet and communicate with
are the sole inspiration of
my work.

WIDOW WOMAN, 24"x36"

james watkins

. . . My personal expression and image is in the romantic realist idiom. I seek to enhance and to impart its significance to mankind in expressing the fertility that takes shape around to oppressed and picturesque people of the world.

It is gratifying to draw from the substance of its productivity that is inclusive of this broad scope.

william curtis

. . . I feel like most black artists today, that social awareness and group consciousness can be combined with creative vision and a personal manner. The everyday living of our people is so evident that one's lifetime could be spent discovering and re-discovering these creative transformations.

In order to communicate to the masses I choose the realistic approach of a Motley using symbolism as a key to identify. With the upward thrust for Black Identity and awareness one cannot help but be spiritually involved and as an artist depict in the boldest terms the events, emotions, frustrations and general moods of the moment.

RIOT: USA, 1968, oil, 39"x50"

willie f. longshore

GLORIA, 1960, pastel, 19"x25"

. . . Black art reveals itself honorably or as a grotesque
distortion of the artist's heritage, and his relationship
to contemporary society.

The black artist has a preoccupation with subject
matter in its representational form; often the subject
is distinguishably divorced from his total
composition.

My art involves painting and photography as basic
communicative tools. Communication suggests an
interaction between the artist and the public in
general. The artist discovers new and better ways of
imparting his ideas about the times in which he lives
and the events resulting from his involvement.

In recent years there has been a re-evaluation of the
camera as an instrument for creative expression.
This is partly due to the new emphasis on the
importance of the tools used in art divorced from
subject matter emphasis. . . .

The camera serves as an adjunct and extension for
my art since I have retained an emphasis on the
importance of the subject.

marva cremer

. . . The substance of my work deals with realities within reality. I seek to rearrange or displace images and events in our world to form disconnected patterns and reflections of thought. I am particularly concerned with those images derived from my dreams and subsconscious childhood experiences.

STRANGE JOURNEY, lithograph

DO YOU KNOW WHAT I'M DOING?
lithograph

david c. driskell

STILL LIFE WITH GATELEG TABLE, mixed media, 36"x48"

. . . I am concerned with what medium can best say the things I want to get across to my
viewers. Therefore, I have selected several to help toward accomplishing this goal. Art, for me,
remains a personal reaction to the world of experiences but I am equally interested in others
sharing the final statement that I make in painted form. In this way I am able to reach to
different things through many approaches to the medium.

As an artist, I feel deeply committed to the idea of shaping content the way I like it.
I am seldom at home imitating form as I see it in the natural order.

95

hayward l. oubre

. . . Writing about one's own work is most
difficult, the simple reason being that an
artist is always eager to know what
the spectator's reaction will be
to his creation.

RAM, graphite, 20"x8"

PROPHET

lois mailou jones

. . . Mine is a quiet exploration—a quest for new meanings in color, texture and design. Even though I sometimes portray scenes of poor and struggling people, it is a great joy to paint.

Hatian Scene

MARCHE'-HAITI, 1965, acrylic, 19"x24"

ron adams

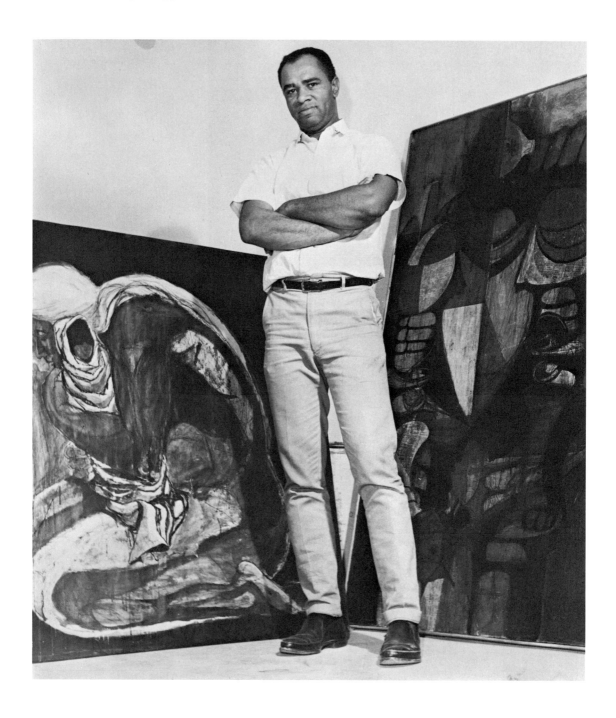

. . . I feel what I have to say as an artist has more meaning to me and my fellow man than any
other contribution I could possibly make. What I have expressed thus far through my art are
my personal feelings of man's inhumanity to man through the symbolic use of the figure
of universal man.

Drawing, 1967

Drawing, 1967

100

david hammons

. . . I feel it my moral obligation as a black artist, to try
to graphically document what I feel socially.

AMERICA THE BEAUTIFUL
body print

AMERICAN HANG UP
body print

eugenia v. dunn

. . . As an aspiring painter,
my primary quests are:
1. Meaning of the universe
2. Seeking universality in
   communication through
   both art and science.
3. Achieving the understanding
   to live and help both myself
   and my fellow man.
4. To sustain the strength to
   be courageous and to share,
   through art, experiences
   in these pursuits with
   others.

BRUSH FIRE OVER ARKANSAS, 1964, 20"x24"

west gale

. . . The woman that my mother worked for asked her one day what I liked to do, whereupon my mother replied, "Oh he doesn't like to do anything but draw."

The woman told my mother to encourage me and from that day on, she did just that even though drawing, at the time, seemed nothing but a waste of time for a black boy. Wasn't it well known that artists are lazy, crazy, and never make a living except, maybe, some overpriced artist like Picasso? Today, though she is recently gone, I am extremely grateful to have had her for my mother, for she gave me respect and encouragement to aspire to be a good artist.

yvonne cole meo

. . . Dynamic movement and a three-dimensional sculptural quality
are inherently a vital part of all my works as I feel that all life occupies
space and has a pulse or beat of its own.

My subject matter ranges from documentary paintings commenting
on human pathos and man's lost identity, as exemplified in my sterile
robotic assemblage, "Automation," and man's aspiration and desires
as depicted in "Contemplation," to earthy and celestial phenomena
typified in "God's Little Acre" and "Omega." I am experimenting with
industrial synthetic materials and their application to the fine arts media
of assemblages and paintings.

AUTOMATION

NO WAY OUT

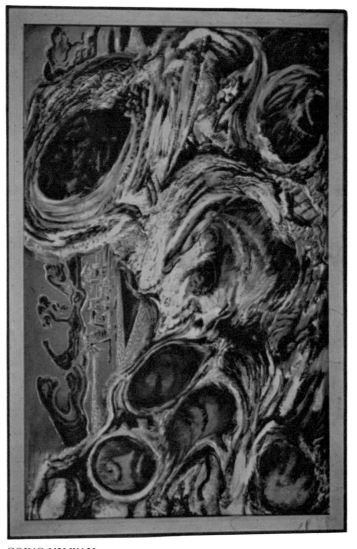

GOING MY WAY

106

. . . We all know that art is not an end in itself, but a means of addressing humanity in a very personal way—for the artist. We are all trying in some way to make our statement. It is not often that I put mine in print.

When starting to work on a painting or construction, I generally have some concept of what I want to do. This concept may or may not be fairly vague. When gradually moving the media around in various forms until the idea becomes solidified, emotional involvement is intensified. Then I must reach a pitch of disregarding all other influences until a single state of creating evolves into a sense of freedom. I am an impatient painter. I am constantly searching for new forms of personal expression. I must be true to those which move me to work. Forcing work along the lines of another's method or style without empathy for it is not really doing your "thing" as the students would say and the work remains cold and uncommunicative.

It is a question of development and transformation that I am constantly concerned with. Development is important. Being a full time instructor and a diligent housewife leave much time for development. It leaves much time for disquieting reflections on your limitations and functions in the art world other than teaching. However teaching is a gratifying experience for me. To work with young people and see their eyes open to the possibilities of visual expression is an important fulfillment.

eva hamlin miller

jewel w. simon

. . . I like to look at the new, the wildly "far out"
creative art, but execute what I consider more
enduring, quiet comments on the social scene . . .

THE EARLY BIRDS, oil, 24"x30"

ALTERNATIVE, 1968, intaglio, 28"x38"

marion epting

. . . To find yourself attempting to defend one side or the other of a dualism is to find yourself in a position that is uncomfortable, confining, limiting, prejudicial, impossible to maintain, and dishonest.

Dualisms, or what may be referred to as examples of the operation of the "rule of two" are, by their nature and definition, situations which are potentially conflicting.

THE MOON ALSO RISES, oil, 5'x5'

POEM, intaglio, 28"x38"

110

UNTITLED, 1968
collage, 40"x46"

dan concholar

. . . I like to think that the colors I use, the subtle; then changes, the texture, the brush work
are intense and yet subtle then sometimes opposed by some area or areas of sharp contrast.
If I can, I like to throw the viewer off balance and at the very same time pull him into
the work itself. But this requires an active participation by the viewer. He must have a
certain willingness to become involved. The viewer cannot just sit on the sidelines and
observe; he can't see anything from there.

I don't like the idea of people approaching my art with the attitude that I am to perform
for them, as if to say "All right, I'm here, let me see what you can do." When you do this,
you are approaching art with a foregone conclusion and anything that does not fit,
you cannot respond to or relate with. There are no preconceived conclusions in art,
nor should there be because then we would cease to move forward creatively. I do
feel that art is an extension of a tradition, of the first time man gazed on chaos and asked
the question, "Who am I? What am I?" Essentially, the art of the Renaissance or today
is no better than that done by the caveman. We may have new tools, new materials and
philosophies, but the expression then was just as strong, just as true and just as meaningful
as the art of today.

I pursue this reality in my own way, perhaps not as different in approach or style as some
other artist, but I believe that whatever direction I move in is something essential to me as
a being and as an artist.

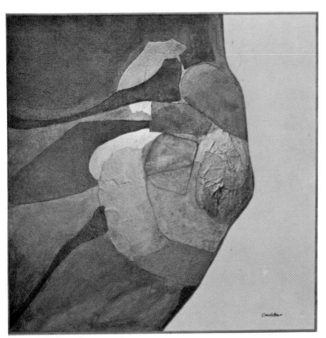

IN YOUR WOMB, 1969
mixed media, 40"x40"

WAR MACHINE, 1968
mixed media, 36"x48"

112

samella s. lewis

. . . Art for me offers an avenue for examining
and exploring ideas for the creation of new
and different form concepts—concepts
that relate directly to my experience and
the world in which I live.

CANEFIELD, serigraph

113

BURNING BUSH, 1964, oil, 24"x30"

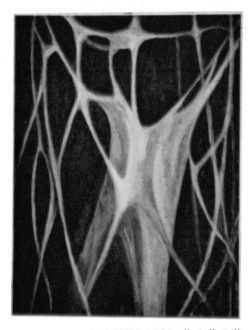

BANYON, 1965, oil, 40"x50"

CITY, oil, 40"x50"

FRUIT, 1968, oil, 34"x50"

ruth g. waddy

. . . Occasionally I find a subject to paint or print that is color, whimsey, joy, not happiness. I feel that happiness is a cultivated, social condition which may forego joy that is visited upon the simple (uncompounded, without sublety) minded. However, more often than not, my subjects are social, evoking I hope, an emotional reaction from the viewer. Only on continued viewing does he become aware of line and color.

PASTORAL, 1966, oil, 36"x46"

DAISIES, 1966, oil, 20"x26"

UNTITLED, 1969, linocut, 10"x20"

THE FENCE, 1969, linocut, 18"x20"

THE KEY, 1969, linocut, 12"x20"

the artists

adams ron

born Detroit, Michigan, 1934; studied at Otis Art Institute in Los Angeles, California, 1965; exhibited in numerous shows in the United States and Mexico.

ballentine jene

born Memphis, Tennesee, 1942; B.A. in architecture from the University of California, Los Angeles, 1964; resides in San Francisco, California.

berry arthur

born Tulsa, Oklahoma, 1923; B.A. from Fisk University, M.A. from Columbia University, 1952, also studied at School of Painting and Sculpture, Skowhegan, Maine; exhibited throughout the United States, numerous one-man shows; teaches at Albany State College, Georgia.

bradford david p.

born Chicago, Illinois, 1937; studied at Chicago Art Institute, Otis Art Institute, Los Angeles, B.S. from Lincoln University, 1963; awards: first place at Missouri State Fair, 1962, Chicago, Illinois, 1968, second place at Atlanta University & National Conference of Artists, 1962; exhibited in group shows at Oakland Museum's New Perspectives in Black Art and Kaiser Center, Oakland, California, 1968.

britt arthur l. sr.

born Cuthbert, Georgia, 1934; studied under Hayward Oubra at Winston-Salem State College, Dr. Tomosa at the University of Japan, Walter Khulmann at the Art Academy, Los Angeles, also other instructor-artists including the University of New Mexico, B.A. and B.S. from Alabama State College, 1959, M.A. from University of New Mexico, 1965; numerous exhibitions and awards including slides at the International Travel Show; presently Acting Chairman of Art Department at Southern University, New Orleans.

brown fred

born Conway, Arkansas, 1941; studied at City College of San Francisco; exhibited in San Francisco at the Blackman's Gallery and the San Francisco Art Festival, 1968.

brownlee henry

born Savannah, Georgia, 1940; studied at Washington School of Art and for two years at Savannah State College; exhibited at Sears Roebuck Art Show and Savannah Art Association's Drawing and Print Competition, 1968; active worker as writer and artist for Southern Christian Leadership Conference.

carraway arthur

born Fort Worth, Texas, 1927; studied at California School of Fine Arts and received Certificate from Academy of Advertising Art, both in San Francisco; numerous exhibitions in oils, watercolor, and graphics (lithographs) since 1953; numerous awards including nomination as one of San Francisco's Future Leaders in the Arts by Committee for San Francisco Future, 1953, Purchase Prize Lithograph and first Prize Lithograph at Los Angeles County Fair Graphic Arts, 1953, Purchase Prize Painting, 1968, Oakland Museum of Art, AWAN Perspectives in Black Art, special scholarship for painting, 1957; collections, Kohler Co., Los Angeles County Art Museum, Oakland Museum of Art, and private collections; traveled all over Africa for two years.

casey bernie

born Wyco, West Virginia, 1939; B.A. in Fine Arts and M.A., 1966 from Bowling Green State University; published in Art News, 1967; exhibited in two one-man shows at the Ankrum Gallery in Los Angeles, two one-man shows at John Bolles Gallery in San Francisco; actively engaged as a screen actor and writer; co-founder of Negro Industrial and Economic Union; president of Community Arts Foundation; star flanker back with the Los Angeles Rams.

chandler dana c. jr.

born Lynn, Massachusetts, 1941; B.S. from Massachusetts College of Art, 1967; exhibited in eight one-man shows, 1967-68 including two at the Boston University Art Gallery, Rhode Island School of Design, innumerable group shows.

coles donald e.

born Philadelphia, Pennsylvania, 1947; studied at Philadelphia College of Art and California College of Arts and Crafts, Oakland, California; exhibited, one-man shows include Associated Students Art Gallery, Oakland, group shows include San Francisco Black Art Fair, Prints and Drawings by California Afro-American Artists, Stanford University, 1969.

concholar dan

born San Antonio, Texas, 1939; studied at Phoenix College and Pasadena City College; exhibited in Arizona State Fair (1st prize, graphics), 1959, Arizona State Fair (1st prize, painting), 1969, Phoenix Art Museum, Udinotti Gallery, Brockman Gallery; principal areas, painting and printmaking; presently, drawing and painting teacher at the Watts Towers Art Center.

cremer marva

born Miami, Florida, 1942; B.A. in Ed., 1965, B.F.A., 1966, M.F.A. (graphic arts), 1968, California College of Arts and Crafts; recipient of William Porter Scholarship, Grace C. Richards Scholarship, graduate half tuition teaching scholarship, California College of Arts and Crafts, 1967; exhibited at two-man show at Western Addition Library, 1968, New Perspectives in Black Art, Kaiser Center, Oakland Museum, 1968, Gallery III, Corte Madera, 1968; currently teaching at Studio I, Oakland California and at the School for Emotionally Disturbed Chicdren, East Bay Activity Center.

crudup doris

born Chicago, Illinois, 1933; studied at Herzl Junior College, Chicago, one year drawing and one year oil painting, 1950-51; exhibited in juried group shows, exhibited at Los Angeles City Hall, 1968.

curtis william

born St. Louis, Missouri, 1939; studied at Lincoln University, 1957-58; exhibited in Paris, 1959-61, Germany, 1963, also exhibited at Atlanta University and Beaux Arts.

d'hue robert raleigh jr.

born Cleveland, Ohio, 1917; studied for six years at Academie Royale des Beaux-Arts, Liege, Belgium, certificate and honors, 1954; exhibited in group and one-man shows in Belgium, France, and the United States; collections, Museum of Liege, Belgium, and private collections all over the world; publications, Wallon Belgian Artists' "Annuaire des Beaux-Arts de Wallonie," 1960, national magazine, United States, 1963; presently art teacher in San Diego Unified Schools.

driskell david c.

born Eatonton, Georgia, 1931; B.A. from Howard University, M.A. from Catholic University of America, 1962, certificates from the Skowhegan School of Painting and Sculpture & Netherlands Institute for the History of Art; all above schooling done on scholarships, grants and fellowships; other grants include European Museum Visitation, Fisk University, Rockefeller Foundation Faculty Research Grant, 1967; exhibited in numerous shows including the Corcoran Art Gallery, National Museum, Rhodes National Gallery, Salisbury, Southern Rhodesia.

dunn eugenia v.

born Henderson, Kentucky, 1918; studied at public schools of Henderson and Louisville, Kentucky, student of Leo Katz, graduate study at Long Island University, 1967-68; exhibited extensively throughout the southeast and middle south; has approximately 300-450 pieces of work in public and private collections; one of the founders and continues very active in The National Conference of Artists.

ensley annette lewis

born Birmingham, Alabama, 1948; self-taught; exhibited in annual community shows and city-wide competition in Barnsdall Park, Los Angeles.

epting marion a.

born Forrest, Missippi, 1940; B.F.A. and M.F.A. from Otis Art Institute, Los Angeles, California; exhibited throughout California; shows include Southern California Exposition (1st place, graphics), Los Angeles City Parks and Recreation (1st place, graphics), First National Print Exposition, Inglewood Art League, Festival in Black, Stanford University, Occidental College, First National Invitational Print Exhibition and others.

fundi ibibio

born Boston, Massachusetts, 1929; B.A., Phi Beta Kappa, from University of California, Berkeley, 1965; exhibited at University of California, Berkeley, during Master's program (graduated with Distinction in Art), and Oakland Museum Show, Perspectives in Black Art.

gale west

born New York, New York; studied at Otis Art Institute, Los Angeles, 1942; has had own gallery, House of Carribean Arts; director of Watts Summer Art Festival, 1963-66; professional dancer and actor.

greene donald o.

born Youngstown, Ohio, 1940; studied at City College of San Francisco, San Francisco Academy of Art, California College of Arts and Crafts; exhibited in many group shows mainly in the Bay area, Oakland Museum Rental Gallery; five year national art film made for educational television, May 1968; extensive experience in youth programs.

green robert h. jr.

born Okmulgee, Oklahoma, 1930; B.A. from Langston University, 1952, M.A. from University of Tulsa, Oklahoma, 1958, Mexico Art School, Juarez, Mexico, additional study and research in Mexican and Indian Arts; exhibited, numerous group and one-man shows, among them, Municipal Gallery, Springfield, Missouri, Wesleyan College, Lincoln, Nebraska, Dallas Museum of Art, Dallas, Texas, Oklahoma Art Center, Oklahoma City, Oklahoma, Denver Museum of Art, Denver, Colorado; recipient of honors from Atlanta University, Topeka City Museum and others, presently, painting and drawing instructor, Alabama State College, Montgomery, Alabama.

howell raymond

born Oakland, California, 1927; self-taught; academic schooling ended with the fifth grade; nationally known and the recipient of many awards.

humphrey margo

born Oakland, California, 1942; studied at Oakland High School, Merritt Junior College (scholarship), California College of Arts and Crafts (scholarship); exhibitions include numerous group shows, and one-man show, Casa de Ena Gallery, 1965, two-man show, Western Addition Library, San Francisco, 1968, Lytton Savings and Loan Association Show, Oakland, 1968, New Perspectives in Black Art, Oakland Museum (two awards), 1968; represented in numerous private and public collections; member of Art-West Associated, North.

johnson marie e.

born Baltimore, Maryland; B.A. from Morgan State College, 1952, M.A. from San Jose State College, 1968; recipient of fellowship to Stanford University in art education, 1968-69; exhibitions include many group and one-man shows including National Academy, Allied Artists of America Annual, NYC, San Francisco Art Museum, California Palace of Legion of Honor, Gumps Gallery, San Francisco, California State Fair, New Perspectives in Black Art, Oakland Museum at Kaiser Center, 1968, one-man shows include Northwood and Polaris Buildings, Fairbanks Alaska, San Jose State College Gallery, San Jose Art Center, Labaudt Gallery San Francisco; recipient of California State Fair non-purchase award, 1962, honorable mention at New Perspectives in Black Art, 1968, work purchased by San Francisco Art Commission; fifty paintings in private collections; presently art instructor in Black Art History, California College of Arts and Crafts, Oakland, California, and consultant to the Oakland Museum of Art, Oakland, California.

jones lois mailou

born Boston, Massachusetts; B.A. from Museum of Boston Fine Arts School, 1927, on four year scholarship; exhibited in over 30 group and 20 one-man shows, including Societe des Artistes, Soulanges Galerie, Paris, France, Corcoran Gallery, Smith-Mason Gallery of Art in Washington, D.C.; awards and honors include first prize, Corcoran Gallery, Washington, D.C., 1953, decorated by President of Haiti for "Achievement in Art," represented in 16 permanent collections in the U.S. and abroad; published, Cedric Dover's American Negro Art, Ebony, 11, 1968 among many others; presently Professor of Design and Watercolor, Howard University, since 1962 conducts student art tours for Howard University to Europe.

jordan jack

born Wichita Falls, Texas, 1925; B.A. from Langston University, 1948, M.A. from Iowa University, 1949, and M.F.A. from State University of Iowa, 1953; exhibited in 23 states, 21 one-man shows; 30 art awards and numerous cash commissions; exhibited in many traveling shows, nationally and internationally; published, Print Portfolio by National Conference of Artists, Prints by American Negro Artists by the Cultural Exchange Center, and others; presently Professor of Art at Southern University, New Orleans; appointed to State of Louisiana Commission of Creative and Performing Arts.

kolawole l. compton

born Beaumont, Texas, 1931; studied at California School of Fine Arts, San Francisco; employed at the San Francisco Museum of Art; academic honors, scholarship student for three years at the California School of Fine Arts, San Francisco Chronicle Certificate of Merit for Sculpture, 1949, other awards, 1954-55; among publications, American Negro Art by Cedric Dover, 1960, Art News & New York Times, 1957, Prints by American Negro Artists by Cultural Exchange Center, 1965, Galeriespiegel Nr: 1-4, 1968, Art Magazine, "Kunst," 1969; exhibited in numerous shows, including USA National Shows, San Francisco Museum (cash prize), 1953, group shows at galleries in New York as well as one-man shows, 1956-63, group and one-man shows in Los Angeles, 1965, in Frankfurt, Stuttgart, and Munich, 1966-67, three-man show in Lagos, Nigeria, 1967, one-man shows at Schrag, Kleine galleries, 1968; lives and works at present in Paris and Munich.

grigsby eugene

born Greensboro, North Carolina, 1918; B.A. from Morehouse College (with Hale Woodruff), 1938, M.A. from Ohio State University, 1940, Ph.D. from New York University, 1963, also studied at American Artists School, New York City, awarded honorary D.F.A. from Philadelphia College of Art, 1964; recipient of Medallion of Merit (one of 25), Gallery of Art, Washington D.C., 1966; taught (as one of six from America) for the Museum of Modern Art at the Brussells World Fair, Belgium, 1958; exhibitions include one-man shows at Phoenix Art Center, 1955, Luxembourg, 1944, Morehouse College, 1967, J. C. Smith University, 1966, Texas Southern University, 1966; publications include "Art Education at Carver High School," Art Education Journal, May 1954, "Teaching Children Art at the Brussells World Fair," Bulletin of the Pacific Arts Association, Fall 1958, "African Arts," The Heard Museum, Phoenix, Arizona; presently Associate Professor in the School of Fine Arts, Arizona State University.

hall wes

born Toledo, Ohio, 1934; studied at Toledo Museum of Art School, University of California, Los Angeles, and Art Center School of Design, B.A. from California State College, Los Angeles, 1960; exhibited in innumerable juried group and one-man shows; many awards and honors; work in permanent collections of both public institutions and private individuals; presently design illustrator with Vignette Films, Los Angeles.

hammons david

born July 24, 1943, Springfield, Illinois; studied at Los Angeles City College, Los Angeles Trade Technical College, Chouinard Art Institute, Otis Art Institute; exhibited, Inglewood Library, Laguna Beach Art Association, National Council of Jewish Women; published, Wilson Library Bulletin; lectured, Dominguez State College

hampton phillip j.

born Kansas City, Missouri, 1922; M.F.A. from Kansas City Art Institute, 1952, also studied at, among others, Drake University; exhibited nationally and internationally; awarded Outstanding Teacher of the Year and Life Membership in National Educational Association, 1965, E. Harris Harbison and Norman O. Houston Purchase Award, among many others; published, American Negro Art by Cedric Dover, 1961, Register of U.S. Living Artists, 1968.

harris john t.

born, 1908; resides in Philadelphia, Pennsylvania; B.Ap.A. from Philadelphia College of Art, 1943, M.A. from Temple University, Tyler; exhibited extensively including Pennsylvania Academy of Fine Arts, Atlanta University, Morgan State College; presently Associate Professor of Art at Cheyney State College.

hayden kitty l.

born Marlin, Texas, 1942; studied four years at Dorsey High School Adult Classes and one and one half years at B.J. Shyffer Workshop, Los Angeles; won numerous awards in local shows; work in several private collections.

hicks leon n.

born Deerfield, Florida, 1933; B.S. from Kansas State University, M.A. and M.F.A. from State University of Iowa, Stanford University, 1964 and La Romita School of Art, Italy, 1966; exhibited in over 30 one-man, two-man and groups shows throughout the U.S., including Des Moines Annual Exhibit, American Graphic Workshops, Cincinnati Art Museum, Ninth Annual Arts Guild Exhibition, Tuskegee Institute, Annual Academy of Design Exhibition, New York, Northwest Printmakers 39th International Exhibition, Seattle Museum, 6th Annual Exhibition of the National Conference of Artists; published, Prints by American Negro Artists, Cultural Exchange Center, Los Angeles, California, The Art Gallery Magazine, 1968; presently art instructor at Lincoln University, Jefferson City, Missouri.

lark raymond

born Philadelphia, Pennsylvania, 1939; studied at Philadelphia Museum School of Art, and degree from Temple University; began study of art the the age of nine, has had instruction in all fields of art, fine and commercial; exhibited throughout the United States in one-man and group shows, often headlining group shows; at age 26, Lark was one of a few artists chosen from California for the Art Event of the Year (Picasso headlined this show), 1966; published, Los Angeles Times Calendar, 1967-68, Symbol Magazine, 1967, Westways Magazine & California Entertainment Guide, 1968; president of Art-West Associated.

longshore willie f.

born Roanke, Alabama, 1933; B.F.A. from Miami University, 1956, and M.A. from Kent State University, 1963; exhibited, one-man and group shows (three or less) Ohio Museum, 1960-68, first award in painting Lima Ohio Museum May Show, 1963, and many college and university galleries; publications, two-page reporduction of paintings in Western Artist Magazine, May 1965; presently art instructor at Lincoln University, Jefferson City, Missouri.

lewis samella s.

born New Orleans, Louisiana; B.S. from Hampton Institute, M.A. and Ph.D. from Ohio State University; recipient of Delta Sigma Theta Scholarship (Dillard University), Curr Scholarship (State University of Iowa), Hampton Insitiute Art Scholarship, American University Scholarship (Ohio State University), Fulbright Grant for Far Eastern Research and Travel, New York State-Ford Foundation Grant (Chinese Art History, New York University), N.D.E.A. Post Doctoral Grant (Chinese Language and Civilization) 2½ years; permanent collections, many including, Baltimore Museum of Fine Arts, Virginia Museum of Fine Arts, High Museum of Atlanta, Ohio Union Gallery, Viktor Lowenfeld Memorial Gallery at Pennsylvania State University, Atlanta University Museum of Contemporary Art, Denison University, Hampton Institute, Boys College, Amon, Jordan; currently Associate Professor in the School of Humanities and Fine Arts at California State College, Dominguez Hills, California; represented by the Ankrum Gallery, Los Angeles, California; co-editor of BLACK ARTISTS ON ART.

mann david

born Los Angeles, California, 1927; studied at Art Student League, New York, University of Mexico, Mexico City, Art Center School, Los Angeles; artist also attended U.S. Merchant Marine Academy; exhibited in DeYoung Museum (purchase award), San Francisco All-City Art Festival, 1960, Seattle Biennial Show (first award, oil), 1962, three times in the Watts Summer Art Festival, Ecumenical Center at University of Southern California, University of California, Los Angeles and Berkeley, Palos Verde Galleria, Palos Verde, California; presently art instructor with Los Angeles Teen Posts.

mason phillip lindsay

born St. Louis, Missouri, 1939; studied at California College of Arts and Crafts; won four gold medals and three place awards while in high school but was unable to accept partial tuition art scholarship at the University of Kansas due to financial condition, so after graduation from high school, spent four years in the Navy; the first painting sold was purchased by the Oakland Museum to hang in the permanent collection; listed in Archives of American Art; published, Sepia Magazine, 10, 1968; presently art instructor in Walnut Creek, California.

maxwell william

born Los Angeles, California, 1934; B.A. from California State College, and M.A. from California State College, 1966, studied under Hudson Roysher and taught part-time at California State College; member of Southern California Designer Craftsmen; exhibited in group show at Ankrum Gallery, Los Angeles, design shows at the Pasadena Science and Industry Museums; presently designs for the trade and teaches at All Nations Settlement House.

meo yvonne cole

born Seattle, Washington; studied at University of California, Los Angeles, B.A. and M.A. from California State College, also studied with Dr. Glenn Lukens, Francis de Erdeley, Herbert Jepson and others; exhibited in numerous juried group shows, among them, Ankrum Gallery, Oakland Art Museum, Leipsig, Germany, Graphic Print Show, Soviet Union, Westwood Art Association, one-man shows include Fisk University, Safety Savings and Loan, Los Angeles, United Design Associates, Beverly Hills; citations and awards include first in Los Angeles Regional Art Exhibit, 1968; published, The International Book Art Exhibits Catalogue, 1965, Prints by American Negro Artists by Cultural Exchange Center, Art Forum, 1965; presently art instructor in Los Angeles secondary schools.

miller eva hamlin

born Brooklyn, New York; B.F.A. from Pratt Institute, 1940, and M.A. from Columbia University, 1945, also postgraduate study at Graduate School of Fine Arts in Florence, Italy; exhibited in numerous group and one-man shows particularly in the Carolinas and east coast of the U.S.A.; designed stained glass window installed 1961 at St. James Presbyterian Church (18'x5'); presently Associate Professor of Art at A and T College, Greensboro, North Carolina.

montgomery evangeline j.

born New York City, 1933; studied at Los Angeles City and State Colleges with Mary Jane Leland, weaving, Hudson Roysher, metal smithing, and California College of Arts and crafts in San Francisco; exhibited in many group shows in jewelry and other crafts and media in Los Angeles, Cambridge, Boston, San Francisco Bay area; many awards including Merit Award in Jewelry at San Francisco Art Festival, 1968, Oakland Museum Purchase of two photographs from New Perspectives in Black Art Show, 1968, Print in juried Graphic Art Show which toured the Soviet Union, 1966; special consultant to Oakland Museum Art Division; founder of Art-West Associated North Inc.; member of Metal Arts Guild of California, National Conference of Artists and other organizations. B.F.A. from California College of Arts and Crafts, 1969; member of Contemporary Art Committee and The Oakland Museum Art Guild, 1969.

mosely jimmie

born Lakeland, Florida, 1927; B.A. from Texas Southern University, 1952, M.A. from Pennsylvania State University, 1955; exhibited in innumerable shows, especially in the states that border the East coast of the U.S.; has won awards each year since 1954; published, Prints by American Negro Artists by Cultural Exchange Center in Los Angeles; presently in 16th year as Director of Art Education at Maryland State College; president of the National Conference of Artists.

mc gaugh lawrence

born Newton, Kansas, 1940; plans to attend San Francisco Art Institute, 1969; self-taught; exhibited in the Bay area and in the Oakland Museum Show, New Perspectives in Black Art.

mc neil william

born Austin, Texas, 1935; B.F.A. from Chouinard Art Institute, 1963, teaching credential from University of Southern California, 1966, M.S., 1968; exhibited in Los Angeles Art Association Print Show, 1965, Brand Library of Art and Music, Glendale, California, 1965, one-man shows at Frye Art Museum, Seattle, The Ryder Gallery, Los Angeles; published, Prints by American Negro Artists by Cultural Exchange Center, 1965; honors, Outstanding Fine Arts Major voted by faculty of Chouinard Art Institute; presently art instructor in Los Angeles public school system.

oubre hayward l.

born New Orleans, Louisiana; B.A. from Dillard University, M.F.A. from University of Iowa; exhibited in innumerable shows throughout the U.S., from Walker Art Center in Minneapolis, Minnesota to the John and Mable Ringling Museum in Sarasota, Florida, Northwest Printmakers Exhibit in Seattle, Washington to Issac Delgado Museum in New Orleans, from an invitational two-man show at Art Directions Gallery in New York City to Carver Museum with prize winning paintings and prints at Tuskegee Institute; published, Cedric Dover's American Negro Art, 1961, A New Direction in Intaglio by Walker Art Center, Design Magazine, 1962 and 1968, designed and copyrighted colorwheel, 1962 and colorchart, 1966, many other reviews and write-ups in art magazines; honors and awards, won every year since 1947 for paintings, prints, sculpture (both plaster and wire); presently Chairman of Art Department at Winston-Salem State College.

outterbridge john wilfred

born Greenville, North Carolina, 1933; self-taught to a great degree; studied at American Art Academy, Chicago, Illinois and Art Center School of Design, Los Angeles; exhibited in Pasadena Artists Association, second award, 1967, Westwood Art Association, best in show and first award in contemporary sculpture, certificate of merit, Authors Study Club, photographed publication by Long Beach Museum, Sixth California Exhibition of Painting and Sculpture (juried by Clement Greenberg).

pajaud william

born New Orleans, Louisiana, 1925; studied at Chouinard Art Institute, Los Angeles, B.A. from Xavier University, New Orleans; exhibited in many group and one-man shows including Los Angeles County Art Museum, Crocker Gallery, Sacramento, De Young Museum, San Francisco, Esther Robles Gallery, Los Angeles; awards, Atlanta University Annual, Westside Jewish Community Center Annual; work in important private collections; member of Society of Graphic Designers, California Watercolor Society and Los Angeles Art Association.

parks james dallas

born St. Louis, Missouri, 1907; B.S. from Bradley University, 1927, M.A. from University of Iowa, 1943; exhibited in one-man shows at Lincoln University, University of Iowa, Fisk University, and many others mainly at universities and colleges in southern and middle western states; awards, Kansas City Art Institute Show, National Conference of Artists Shows, 1962 and 1963, and others; published, American Negro Art by Cedric Dover, Negro Art and Music by Lindsay; permanent collections, Lincoln, Howard and Texas Southern Universities, Springfield City Art Museum; exhibited in group shows at St. Louis City Art Museum, Joslyn Museum, Omaha, Nebraska, Illinois State Fair; presently Chairman of Art Department, Lincoln University, Jefferson City, Missouri.

perkins angela l.

born Chicago, Illinois, 1948; A.A. in psychology from Los Angeles City College, self-taught as artist; exhibited in Watts Summer Festival, 1967 and 1968, Art-West Associated Inc., Independent Square Qualifying Exhibit, 1968.

perry michael kavanaugh

born Los Angeles, California, 1940; B.F.A. from Otis Art Institute, M.F.A. from Otis Art Institute, 1967; exhibited in Otis Art Institute Alumni Exhibition, Independence Square Qualifying Show, Los Angeles City Hall Rotunda, 1968; permanent collection, Golden State Mutual Life Insurance Company, presently art instructor at Albany State College, Albany, Georgia.

reid william

born Raleigh, North Carolina, 1927; self-taught; exhibited in the Watts Summer Festival, Los Angeles, California, 1968.

rickson gary a.

born Boston, Massachusetts, 1942; self-taught; very active in the art community, one of the original founders of the Boston Negro Artist Association and first president, founder of Annual Outdoor Arts Festival, cultural chairman of Malcolm X Foundation, Boston, Massachusetts, organizer of Black Art, Boston, Massachusetts; exhibited widely and continuously, nationally and internationally; travelled throughout Europe and the Soviet Union with Graphics by American Negro Artists Show sponsored by Soviet-American Relations, 1966.

roberts lucille d.

born Hyattsville, Maryland; A.B. from Howard University, and A.M. in Fine Arts from University of Michigan; exhibited in group and one-man shows including Society of Washington Artists, Smithsonian Institute, College Museum, Hampton Institute, Hampton, Virginia, Washington Gallery of Art, Dickey Gallery at Washington, D.C. Teachers College, 1968; honors and awards, Agnes Meyer Fellowship, 1963, Evening Star Award, Society of Washington Artists, 72nd Annual Show, 1966; paintings on loan to the U.S. State Department's "Art in the Embassies Program" in the U.S. Embassies in Karachi, Pakistan, and Taipei, Taiwan; travelled in Canada, Europe, Mexico and Africa; presently Assistant Professor of Fine Arts, Teachers College, District of Columbia.

rogers brenda

born Los Angeles, California, 1940; B.S. from University of Southern California, 1963; exhibited in Simon Rodia Festival of the Arts, merit award, 1967, purchase award, Multipurpose Health Center, 1967; presently teacher in Los Angeles public school system.

rogers charles d.

born Cherokee, Oklahoma, 1935; B.A. from California State College, 1963, majored in art history; exhibited in many group shows including Art-West Associated juried shows at Los Angeles City Hall Rotunda, one-man shows include Dooto's Music Center, Security Pacific National Bank, 1964; published, Prints by American Negro Arts by Cultural Exchange Center; graphics exhibited travelled in Soviet Union; also exhibited at University of California, Los Angeles; presently art instructor with Teen Posts.

saar betye

born Los Angeles, California; B.A. from University of California, Los Angeles; exhibited extensively in group one-, two-, and three-man shows including Los Angeles County Art Museum, San Francisco Legion of Honor Museum, Northwest Printmakers, Seattle, Washington, 20th National Print Exhibit, Library of Congress, Washington, D.C.; published, Prints by American Negro Artists by Cultural Exchange Center, 1965, Art Gallery Magazine, 4, 1968; many permanent collections and private collections throughout the U.S.A.; won many local and national awards.

simon jewel w.

born Houston, Texas, 1911; B.S. summa cum laude, from Atlanta University, major in mathematics at age of 19, B.F.A. from Atlanta School of Art, 1967; also studied under Hale Woodruff and Alice Dunbar at Spelman College (AU); first Negro graduate from Atlanta School of Art, of many first in artist's career; exhibited since 1934, nationally and internationally; many honors, prizes, and awards; work in world-wide collections, private and institutional; published, American Negro Art by Cedric Dover, Prints by American Negro Artists by Cultural Exchange Center, Los Angeles, California, Registry of Living Artists.

taylor della brown

born Charleston, West Virginia, 1922; B.S. from West Virginia State College, M.A. from Boston University, 1945, also studied at Boston Museum School of Art, Massachusetts College of Art, McGill French Summer School; exhibited in Boston Museum of Fine Arts, Art Exhibit for Dedication of Charleston Civic Center, Kanawha County Centennial Exhibition, first prize, ceramics, 1963, 31st Allied Artists Exhibition, first prize, ceramics, and other exhibits and awards; published, poetry, "Aurorals Gift," Negro Digest, 9, 1965, American Society of African Culture Newsletter, 3, 1965, "Reflections on West African Art", art reviews, book reviews, Charleston Gazette and Gazette/Mail; travelled in Europe, 1958, in Europe and West Africa, 1964, Dakar, Senegal, 1966, Haiti, 1968; membership includes American Craftsman's Council and National Conference of Artists; presently Professor of Art, West Virginia State College and art critic for Charleston Gazette and Gazette/Mail.

taylor rod a.

born Washington, D.C., 1932; studied at Virginia State College, American University (graduate work in sculpture), Howard and Catholic Universities (sculpture and ceramics); exhibited in many shows including Smithsonian Institute, Washington, D.C., 1964-65, Corcoran Art Gallery, Washington, D.C., 1965, Catholic and Howard Universities, 1967, Smith Mason International Gallery, Washington, D.C., The Little Art Gallery, Raleigh, N.C., 1968; prizes and awards, Saratoga Springs Art Fair, first prize, 1964, Creative Crafts Exhibition, Smithsonian Institute, 1964, third prize, sculpture, Smithsonian Institute, 1964, honorable mention, Atlanta University Annual Show, 1965, first prize, Scan Art Fair, Washington, D.C., 1966, and others.

towns elaine

born Los Angeles, California, 1937; B.A. from University of California, Los Angeles, 1960, majoring in art, minor anthropology, M.A., 1962, majoring in art, minor social sciences; exhibited in Los Angeles County Museum, 1960, one-man exhibit, Safety Savings and Loan Association, 1961, Masters Exhibit, University of California, 1962, James Phelan Award Travelling Exhibit, 1963, Exposion de Artistas Becarios Fulbright, Madrid, 1964, Exhibition of Prints by American Negro Artists, sponsored by the Institute of Soviet-American Relations in the Soviet Union, 1966-67, Los Angeles City Schools Artmobile Exhibit, 1968-69; awards, Fulbright Grant to Spain, 1963-64; travelled in Paris, Rome and Florence.

vaughn h. royce

born Cleveland, Ohio, 1930; B.A. in art history (minor, religion and Spanish) on four year scholarship from Princeton University, B.A. in art from San Francisco State College, 1967; exhibited in Walnut Creek Art Center and Oakland Museum New Perspectives in Black Art, 10, 1968; awards, work purchased by Oakland Museum and San Francisco Art Commission, 10, 1968, nomination to $10,000 Danforth Foundation Fellowship for Graduate Study, University of California, Los Angeles, 1958; presently project director of ABLE (The Arts and Business Experiences), San Francisco State College.

waddy ruth g.

born Lincoln, Nebraska, 1909; studied at Famous Artists Home Study Course, Los Angeles City College, Los Angeles County Otis Art Institute; exhibited in group and one-man shows including Jimmy Crawford's Frame Shop, Los Angeles, 1964, Safety Savings and Loan Association, Los Angeles, 1965, Internationale Buchkunst-Aussellung Leipzig, 1965, Los Felis Jewish Community Center, Los Angeles, 1965, Jewish Women's Council House, Black Dialogue, 1968-69, AWA Negro History Week at Los Angeles City Hall, 1963-68, New Perspectives in Black Art, Kaiser Center, Oakland, 1968; founder of Art-West collected prints for the book, "Prints by American Negro Artists," published by the Cultural Exchange Center, Los Angeles, California, and on west coast for exhibition in Moscow, Leningrad, Alma Ata, and Baku, USSR, 1966; co-editor of BLACK ARTISTS ON ART.

walker larry

born October 22, 1935; B.S. in Ed. and M.A. from Wayne State University, Detroit, Michigan; exhibited in over 60 juried exhibitions, over 15 group exhibitions, over 11 one-man shows; collections include University of the Pacific, Pioneer Museum and Haggin Art Galleries, Detroit Board of Education, Merced Art Association, Office in Washington, D.C. of California Councilman John McFall, and numerous private collections throughout the United States; presently Associate Professor of Art, University of the Pacific, Stockton, California.

washington mary parks

born Atlanta, Georgia; A.B. from Spelman College, 1946, studied under Hale Woodruff, also studied at Art Students League under Reginald Marsh and the University of Mexico, D.F.; exhibited widely; presently art instructor in secondary schools in San Jose, California.

watkins james

born Macon, Georgia, 1925; studied at Society of Arts and Crafts, Detroit, Michigan, 1949-52; exhibited at the Atlanta University Annual from the 16th through the 22nd Exhibition winning top purchase, honorable mention, or popularity award each time, one-man show, Akron Art Institute, Akron, Ohio, Beaux Art Guild, Tuskegee, Alabama, Emancipation Proclamation Art Exhibit, Chicago, Illinois are among other exhibitions; published, Cedric Dover's American Negro Art.

welton roland

born San Francisco, California, 1919; studied at Art Students League, New York City, Otis Art Institute and Chouinard Institute of Fine Arts, Los Angeles; exhibited locally with Art-West Associated at Los Angeles City Hall Rotunda since 1962, Prints by American Negro Artists Exhibition sponsored by Institute of Soviet-American Relations in the Soviet Union and Prague, Czechoslavakia, 1966-67.

white amos

born Montgomery, Alabama; B.S. from Alabama State College, 1958, M.F.A. from University of Southern California, 1961; exhibited widely and continuously including General Motors Fisher Body Design Exhibition, 1951-52, Designer-Craftsman U.S.A., Museum of Contemporary Crafts, New York City, Design West, California Museum of Science and Industry, 1960, Contemporary Design, San Diego County Exposition, Del Mar, California, 18th National Decorative Arts and Ceramics Exhibit, Wichita, Kansas, 1964, Kuhn-White Exhibit, LeMoyne Art Foundation Gallery (two-man show), Tallahassee, Florida, 1965, Florida State Fair Fine Arts (invitational), Tampa, Florida, 1966, Deshaes-White Exhibit (two-man show), University of Jacksonville, Jacksonville, Florida, 1967, Ceramics '68 (one-man show), Alabama State College, Montgomery, Alabama, 1968; honors and awards, many including State Award for Design and Craftsmanship in Automotive Styling and Model Construction, 1951, honorable mention, 1952, ceramic demonstration, Los Angeles County Home Show and Exposition, 1961; member and state representative of American Craftsmen's Council; presently Associate Professor of Art, Florida A & M University.

williams laura w.

born Philadelphia, Pennsylvania, 1915; studied abstract painting under Richard Bowman at Redwood City, California, 1965-68, College of San Mateo, 1960-65; exhibited in The Negro in American Art and New Perspectives in Black Art; received honorable mention in above exhibits, only time artist has exhibited; began art courses as a hobby seven years ago, became absorbed, and has never stopped studying.

wright bernard

born Pittsburgh, Pennsylvania, 1938; self-taught; exhibited extensively in the Los Angeles area and in the Soviet Union, Prague, Czechoslavakia with the Graphics of American Negro Artists Exhibit sponsored by Soviet-American Relations.